I0620585

COMPLETE

and

Soul

ROXSANE K TIERNAN

Copyright 2024 by Roxsane K Tiernan

ISBN: 978-1-966615-17-0 (Paperback)
ISBN: 978-1-961225-89-3 (Hardback)
ISBN: 978-1-961225-90-9 (Ebook)

All rights reserved. This book or any portion thereof may not be reproduced or used in any manner whatsoever without the express written permission of the publisher except for the use of brief quotation in a book review.

CONTENTS

BOOK 1

BOOK 2

BOOK 1

Coquitlam River Morn

LESSON IN LOVE

Learn well this lesson in love
Love is a two-sided affair
Viable only when shared
Sharing the joys and sharing the sorrows
Increasing one's awareness of the effect the world has on others.

Learn well this lesson in love
Learn to talk, talk, talk and listen, listen, listen
Hear the hurt, the impatience and the joy
Understand the gentleness, the compassion, the striving.

Learn well this lesson in love
Learn to encourage—reaching out
Exploring all possible areas of growth
For when something stops growing
It begins to die.

Learn well this lesson in love
Live life to its fullest
Bring home the joy of new found friends
Of accomplishments, of creation.
Learn to stretch, to reach, to be free.

Learn well this lesson in love
Learn to risk, to wonder, to admire

To keep the world fresh at your door
To enjoy the cold and the rain of life
Because it makes the sunshine more.

Learn well this lesson in love
LOVE TO LIVE.

Learn well this lesson in love Learn that love is two-sided
Love needs batting back and forth.
It needs polishing, rearranging and refurbishing.
It can tear you down or build you up.
It requires a constant effort.

Learn well this lesson in love
Learn that love has its costs
The more you invest the more you get back.
Learn to see the love in tasks performed for you The thoughtfulness,
the time, the love.

Silent Sentinels

FEELINGS

I've bottled them up.
I've sealed them in stone.
I don't want my feelings
Let loose on their own.

One Fine Day

HOW TO BE RICH

And this is the way to be rich
To value each minute of every day
To experience the pleasures along the way
A single flower, a cloudy sky, a trio of ducks floating by
To let your heart be taken by storm
To feel the sun's warmth on a wintery morn
To admire the curved branches against the snow
To let your heart go, to let it go
To bask in the glow of a warm hearted greeting
To thoroughly enjoy every chance meeting
To hear the music and quicken your pace
To dance for the joy of it all by yourself
To feel happily tired after working hard
To see the care in a well-kept yard
To understand people far and near
To work for a world free from fear
Yes, this is the way to be rich

Tulip Time

SPRING COLORS

The fluted mauve flowers of the jacaranda tree
Stand out against the sky pleasuring me.
The scent of llamaradas, orange flame flowers on the vine
Make one remember the beautiful and the sublime.
Bright red poinsettias on bushes six feet high,
Doubles and triples astound the passers-by.
Hibiscus flowers lining all the walks,
The yellow, pink, and salmon ones make visitors talk.
The bougainvillea spilling over the garden wall
Magenta, cochineal and sandy peach tumble and sprawl.
These are the flowers of Mexico I love most of all.

Waltz of the Flowers

GRANDMA

Grandma, do you remember?
Yes, I have a son, John.
He lives on the coast somewhere
I haven't seen him for years.
Grandma, where is your trunk?
Oh, yes, I brought you many presents…
The pillow ticking is for you.
I wonder when I will get to John's house…
I have his violin and the china, too.
Grandma, where are you going?
I must see John….I really must.
Can you help me pack?
I need to go…he will be looking for me
Grandma, Dad wants you to stay.
But she was gone.
Gone to search for John—
That other John she could only remember

Wish You Were Here

A MIRROR OF LIFE

Consider yourself a mirror of life
You are.
You reflect the pain and the joy
Of those you care about.
You distort the feelings that hit
Your imperfect surface
Causing defects to be magnified,
Joys shrunk.
The less perfect the mirror
The greater the distortion.
Remember the bent mirrors
In the haunted house.
How easy it is for a twisted personality
To see mainly the sadness
The rain of life
Never reflecting the warmth of the sun.
Don't keep your mirror in the dark
Mirrors don't have light.
They only reflect.
Put your mirror where endless light variations
Are possible
Give your life the depth, the texture
Of maximum exposure.
Then, and only then, can we see life as it is—
Complex and varied.

Remember, you are a mirror of life.
If you are always with sad, narrow people
You will be sadder.
If you are only around the circus
Your reflections will be bizarre.
But think of the wonder, the joy
If you reflect love, magnify peace
So that others, many others
Can reflect and reflect
These joys endlessly.
Remember we are all mirrors of life.

Winter Stream

TOKYO WINTER

It was the cold…
Rubbing against her face
Making the nose snuffly,
the eyes water and vision blur.
It was the cold
that made her lean forward
into the wind
and the fingers to tighten on the
string bag handles.
And then...the wind died
letting the sun's warmth through
letting her straighten, relax
only to be caught by the next gust.
It was the cold
The friction of the wind against the skin.
The blood rushing to the surface,
The burning cold, the unyielding body
shutting out all forms of cold
that Tokyo winter.

Conjunction

PATCHES

Patches of clear blue sky
Patches of life running by
Patches of joy sent from above
Patches on clothes you really love.
Patches that reinforce all creation
Patches of strength, Patches of beauty
Patches on a well worn soul
Patches that keep us together
till we reach our goal.
Patches of light, patches of dark
Patches that are discreet never seen.
Patches of care
Patches rough—even mean
Patches of sun, patches of cloud
Patches of color crying out loud.
Patches fulfilling many a purpose
Creating a quilt of remembrances of life.
Times of joy, times of strife
In these ways and many more
Patches show what life had in store.

Gypsy Creek

IN THE FALL OF MY YOUTH

She was a rebel
She loved to argue
Enchanting some
Entertaining others
And frustrating those close to her.
She loved to talk, to debate, to explore
All avenues of life.
She enjoyed the parry and thrust
The respect, the logic, the challenge.
She would question, probe—
Looking for reasons, for understanding, for acceptance.
She needed the attention, the respect, the power.
She loved the freedom, the lack of jealousy, of incrimination.
It was great to be young,
To sit at the back of the bus
And argue with those old men.
She fascinated them and they looked forward
To the weekly encounters—
Anticipating, waiting, hoping,
Needing the exchange as much as she did.
More color was added to their lives
Another perspective, dimension, focal point.
Forty minutes of life,
A small adventure…
That began and ended at the bus stop,
In the fall of my youth.

Come by Chance

GREEN

Green grass growing by the green fence
Green gingham dress, clean and crisp.
Green salads—fresh, full of crunch.
Green—go. Go, live, get on with it.
Green frog, flopping, hopping, green.
Green trees, giving shade, love.
Green moss, carpet soft, comforting,
GREEN.

Song for the Mountains

BROTHERHOOD OF MAN

You can only live your own life
So live it very well.
You don't know whose life you'll influence—
You really cannot tell.
You can only do your own job.
It is really up to you
much as you think you understand
You can't walk in another's shoes.
So, try to be accepting
Take joy in what people are,
Try positive reinforcement
To brighten another's star.
Try to see the whole picture
the grand, eternal plan—
Remember to add your sparkle
To the brotherhood of man.

Near Moraine Lake

THINK

Think peace
Transmit love.
Gain Knowledge
Spread understanding
Feel compassion
Provide support Think peace
Forge equality.

Cherry Blossom Time

SMALL CHILD

Full of promise, Full of hope
With lots of encouragement
With Life's trials you'll cope
You need to learn
From cause and effect
The flow of nature, a wide scope
Teaches personal respect,
not to sit around and mope.
To solve your own problems
To learn from your mistakes
To always be encouraged to do your personal best
To never rub it in when you've failed a test.
To learn to live with failure,
To accept and then go on.
Living with success
Can make you very, very strong.
To be strong, to be whole—
To reach many a new goal
To be open to the possibilities of life.
This I wish you, Small child.

Weeds and Seeds

NANCY

On that frosty October morn
Two minutes before Nancy was born
"I'm sure it's a boy," the doctor said
But Nancy was there instead
And since that day when Nancy came
Things have never been the same
Her hair's not red, not quite—
Her eyes are blue, sparkling bright.
At seven o'clock, my slippers she brings
As if to say, "Get up, you lazy thing."
She's happy as a lark all day
And loves to play, play, play.
Most of the toys have lost their charms,
Off the duck's head, the doll's arms.
My china is diminishing fast.
I wonder how long this stage will last.
She climbs into the bathroom sink
And chews a bar of soap that's pink.
Into her hair she is combing milk—
Only yesterday it was soft as silk.
Quickly, when everything seems amiss
She turns up her face to offer a kiss.
Now she's on the kitchen table
She makes this house look like a stable
Sometimes I wonder, I must admit—
How I'll ever make a lady out of "it".

Evening in Provence

I WANT...

To visit Guatemala, Costa Rica and Peru
To maybe see Colombia, Ecuador and Chile, too.
Then off to tour Europe—
the castles, the country, the people, the places.
The joy of seeing old friends
And meeting new faces.
I want to have my own school—
An inter-cultural institute,
Where more than just language
Is in hot pursuit.
I want to remodel my house—
The kitchen and bath
To make the garden more like a country path.
Maybe I'd like to learn to sail—
I'm not sure what to avail.
I'd like to explore parts of Africa, too
Burkina Faso, Ivory Coast—even Chad.
Sangam, India and Burma
Might not be too bad.
I've got a strong case of Gypsy
I want to go, to do, and to see.
People and places all over this world fascinate me.
I want to learn the powers of negotiation
To make stronger people, countries and nations.
I want to write books—on child care, on understanding
On struggling with life.
Maybe on why every person needs a VERY good wife
Now that would be fun—
Tongue-in-cheek, not so meek
What else is there I want to seek?
There are lots of things to see, to do, to try—
I really don't want life to pass me by.

Emergence

PURPLE

I have my bug-eye sunglasses
With mauve, metallic frames
I have my purple boots
For aerobics not the rain
Yes, purple is my color
I could write a similar book
But purple as I use it
Is like a fishing hook
It catches your attention
It keeps me current, alert
The communication lines are open
I don't know what the wavelength is
I do know that it works.
There is no generation gap
There's not much they could do
To get me in a flap
The purple boots and glasses
They really set the pace—
They help me set the challenge
For all of us to face.

Wetlands

DETOUR

I bet you've never been on a bus
That travelled thus
Off the main road
Through a dinky little town
Through someone's courtyard
Down the narrow lane
Out through two huge mud holes
To a decent road again.
We often saw the highway
Clogged, so full of cars
Then stands along our smaller road
Selling *licuado* out of jars
This strangely pleasant byway
Gave us a glimpse of rural life.
The detour was quite refreshing
We really didn't mind.
You never knew around what corner
Something fascinating you'd find.
And if when life affords it we detour
Down the track
We often find our perspective changed
When we venture back.
The places we never get to,
The things we never see
Give life a different flavor.
These little intermissions we really should SAVOR!

Heriot Bay

LIFE'S LOOM

What are you working on
On Life's Loom?
Are the colors full of joy,
Sobriety or gloom?
What is the design?
Do you have a precise cartoon?
Are the color changes planned?
Does it suit your "room"?
What have you interwoven
With your carefully chosen threads?
Life needs a resilient fabric
Nothing inflexible or harsh.
You need suppleness and flexibility
Yard after yard.
Perhaps you began with tabby
For life was really black or white
And you needed twill for strength,
Durability is a real delight.
Later on you needed warmth
With interwoven spaces
Double cloth, career and home life
Lead to varied paces, varied faces.
The lace weaves came last
The possibilities are vast
They filter in harmony of light, of peace
So at last the work on our loom can cease.

By the Brunette

TO KNOW YOU

I'd like to know you better
To understand you well
But I'm never sure who's ready
For the things I have to tell.
There's things you want to hear
And things I'd like to say
But the fact they're not the same
May frighten you away.
At times my soul is tormented
At times it's very free.
Are there similar realities
For both you and me?
How have you coped with the dilemmas
Of your own private life?
How do you handle the stress? The strife?
What are your real loves?
What brings you peace?
Where do you find pleasure?
Where release?
Are you complimentary to my nature?
Supplementary or incongruent?
You speak a language in which
I'm not very fluent.

Alouette River

JOURNEY INTO LIFE

In the journey into life we take
Each one starts from a different place.
Each one has his own destination
Each one gets off at a specific station.
And as we travel, our plans may change
There are many options in our lives to arrange.
Some of us travel quickly over by jet
But many of us are not ready for that yet.
Some of us crawl pathetically slow.
We poke and we poke—everywhere we go.
The worlds that we see are never the same
Some seek beauty, others fame.
Some are actively involved, others only look.
Each one of us could write quite a different book
Welcome to my world.

Song for Spring

LOVE

Love—for the blood to rush
Straight through your veins
For your head just to swirl
To be almost insane
For the joy to carry you up,
Up, up to the clouds
For the feeling you want to laugh
Or to cry right out loud.
Love—for its sadness
Its temporary madness
For the merry-go-round
You are on.
For the secret delight
When your heart is in flight
When the love that you share
Seems too strong to bear
And the glow that you feel
Seems too great to be real
For the heady emotions
That sweep like a flood to the oceans.
Love—when the pain that you feel
At another's small sorrows
Makes you want to take them away
For a hundred tomorrows.
All the wrenching, the tearing—
It certainly is wearing.
Love—How long can it last?
When will this feeling be past?
What did I do to deserve it?
And—for goodness' sake—
How can I preserve it?

Moon out of Africa

TO MY HIGHER SELF

What are you doing in the corner?
What are you doing hiding away?
What are you doing in the background?
Get out in front, show me the way!
Why do you stand there in the shadows?
Why are you quiet, meek, and mild?
Why don't you push me down the right path?
Why do you act like a subdued child?
Is it because I am so busy,
Because I never really listen well?
Is it because I do my own thing
And rarely sit and rest for a spell?
Maybe I should take life more slowly—
Maybe I should take the scenic route.
I've always been very curious
I need to know just everything, to boot.
I really want to know what is the right way.
I need to find it on my own.
Can you tell me for which sins in which lifetime
This time I must atone?

The Grove

IT'S MY JOB....

To question, to probe, to challenge, to create
To make a world free from hate
To comfort, to strengthen, to respect old and new
To make friends of many, not just a few,
To study the world, its many faces,
To find the familiar in foreign places,
To enjoy life to its very hilt,
To live a life free from guilt.
To be a symbol of courage, of hope
To never, no, never sit around and mope,
To consider the future, to remember the past,
To believe we can find peace, at last, at last.
To set a goal, to follow it through
And every day to learn something new.
THAT"S my job.

Letters in the Sand

HOW WOULD I LOVE THEE

I'd love thee with the joy of watching a fancy parade.
A parade of experiences that's not easily made
But without the fanfare heard by the crowd
With the Mozart-like music that is never too loud.
I'd love thee with kindness, with gentleness, with hope
With a joy in day-to-day living that never lets you mope.
Spilling patience, encouragement on tremulous fears
Being so crazily happy that you fight back the tears
With unspoken words over distances great
With music and laughter from a previous fate
Still, deep emotions that grab you again
The tugging, the twisting, the innocent pain.
Those feelings, all those feelings, they are on the loose again
How lucky, how curious, how puzzling the mood
The acceptance, the understanding... a shyness—so coy
Can all of this be a response to a middle-aged boy?
Oh, oh crazy love—it happens all the time
That crazy love of mine
Oh, crazy love

Onward and Upward

EXPLORING

Follow the confusing streets of my mind
Down torturous unnamed walkways
Through busy thoroughfares
Taking some crossroads
Missing others
Searching for life, its meaning
Its goals
Out with the busy throngs
Streets teeming with life
Leading to work, to play, to home.
Foreign streets, leading nowhere—
Lost, confused, full of fear
Curiosity leading forward
To finally find a friend.

Warm

ANGER

Suppressed anger,
Slow-cooking, dormant—It lies waiting.
Just waiting for a chance word,
An inflection in another's voice
And out it comes—
Out of all proportion to the event

Tranquility

Patterns

CELEBRATE

Seeing the joy in all creation
Seeing the challenges facing the nation
Seeing the hardships,
the weary, the worn, the beaten
Seeing life take its toll
Seeing success, friendship and love
For all creation
The strong, the weak, the shy, the bold.
Accepting life and carrying on.
Trying to teach people to be positive, strong
Celebrating accomplishments.
Enjoying life!
We have to work to end the strife
And find a way to celebrate life.

Meiji Morning

I ASK YOU

Did you say I could travel?
Well, when can we leave?
What kind of adventure
Do you have up your sleeve?

Rushing Waters

ME

I've always been excited
Nervous, shy, afraid.
I don't know why I'm like that—
Guess it's how I'm made.
I've always been curious
I want to go here and I want to go there.
I ask a lot of questions
At times, that's rather hard to bear.
I want to do this
And I want to do that.
I search and I search
For a solution that's pat.
I travel down the main road
I travel down the byway.
There are many detours on my life's highway.
I've learned a lot of useful things
Useless things and more.
You never know what will come to the fore.
A life of exploration is for sure in store.
My brain works when I'm sleeping—
Sometimes when I'm awake—
You never know which direction
My thoughts will take.

Bab's Bouquet

CRAZY LADY

Weird person, crazy lady
Self-effacing fool
Who am I? What am I?
A drone in the common pool?
Where do I come from?
What do I mean?
Can I contribute to the world scene?
Let it go, let it all show
Cry a lot, sigh a lot…
Open your heart to the world
No one can read a banner
Until it is fully unfurled.

Motoko's Friends

YOUNG WOMEN

Young women
Special young women
From all over the world
Searching for the way
Not any way
But the best way
To develop economic potential,
To use money, resources and people well.
To establish human rights,
To assert them, maintain them
And find PEACE.
Peace which is more,
More than an absence of conflict—
Peace through equality, self-development
And love.

Critical, critical, analytical
I bend, explore
Beseech, implore
What makes my world go 'round?

Life is full of wonder—
The sun, the cold, the birds, the trees—
A child fascinated by a bug in the weeds.

From Zanzibar

STUDENTS

Students, easily embarrassed, searching,
Longing to know, to understand.
Eager to share—their food, their traditions,
With touching gifts, symbols of friendship and caring.
Careful progress, repetition and patience—
With difficult sounds, the tape recorder and me.
Full of kindness, immeasurable kindness—
Love of life and of learning
Students of English, of life and the World.

Blue Lagoon

VACATIONS

Everyone from Who is going to Where
To see what it is the people do over there.
Everyone from Where is going to Who
Everyone, except quite a few.
The people from What are going to Which
In which most of the people are rich
What attracts people to What, I don't know
The only way to find out is to go—
To What!

The Hobbit Tree

FEELINGS

Soft, doe-eyed, gentle—
Confused and hurt and torn—
Caught in a trap of tradition
That pulls and twists you
Night and Morn.
Making you question
Your values, your satisfactions
The love that you've found
And the care
Is anything really wrong
With these wonderful feelings
You share?

Blue Lake

PONDERING

Don't push, don't prod,
Don't reach for the phone.
Some things are better
Left to sort out on their own.
I guess he needs security
He really wants you back.
He can't see how he ever
Got off on the wrong track.
I believe he really loves you
And he's such a wonderful guy
I wonder if you'd make it
If you gave it another try
He's a warm-hearted, people person
Kind and gentle, bold and shy.

Grace's Garden

YOU

I love you, really love you,
I care whether you live or die.
So, I've gone away to give you
Space to grow, to achieve, to try.
When I come back I hope
You've found a little more of yourself
I want to see you busy
Not sitting on a shelf
You've got such possibilities
Potential, talent and more.
You can never tell
What life holds in store.
I want to see you happy
Doing what's good for you.
I want you to make your own decisions,
To yourself be true.
Get out and share your talents
The world is waiting for you.
Yes, YOU

Duelling Dragons

CONTROL

Look carefully at your life and see
See what you really need—
A sense of control
Of power to solve life's crises
Of strength—pure, physical strength.
See what you really want—
Love, unconditional and yielding
Definitely dependent love
Needing you, needing it. See why you live
For others, for their approval
BUT mostly for yourself
For your pleasures, for tomorrow.
See how you live—
Narrowly, cautiously, afraid of the risk
Of trusting others
Of being let down. Afraid of life.
Look carefully at your life.
Is this you?

Heron Haven

THIS VEHICLE

My body, the vehicle of my life force
Carries me onward
Turning every which way—
Sometimes to the left, the logical side.
Often the brakes need adjusting
As I rush pell-mell toward life.
I need something to slow me down.
At times, the oil must be changed-
The exercise necessary for flexibility and a long life
Must be done.
This vehicle needs a protective coating
To keep the skin supple and moist.
It requires high octane fuel—unleaded—
Special nutrition for top performance.
The windows need cleaning of anything
That obscures the vision of a full life.
Others watch the signals for direction
And mood change.
There is no cruise control on this model
Sometimes I proceed too quickly, sometimes too slow.
Because this model has a short wheelbase and front-wheel drive
It handles the curves life throws at it
And navigates through snowstorm after snowstorm.
This vehicle, like any other good possession
Must be carefully maintained.

Aurora

FLYING

Flying
In my mind
Over the ocean
Over the ice flows
Over the volcanic field
Observing life from a distance
Able to see relationships and patterns
Fascinated by the rhythm and flow
Understanding, relating
The rounded, perfect cones of possible volcanoes
With the larger cones of dormant volcanoes
Of seeing lava flows
Pouring onto the surface of the earth
Lava flows cooked in some underground cauldron
Pouring forth when the cauldron can contain them no more.

Forest Monarch

EVENTUALLY

Believe the weather will get better,
It usually does,
Eventually.
Believe life will get better
It usually does
Eventually.
Believe your friends will understand you,
They usually do,
Eventually.
Try to get physically fit
You can
Eventually.
Try to live life well
You will
Eventually.
Try to see the positive side
You will
Eventually.
Try to find your niche in life
You will
Eventually.

November

WHY WE WEEP

Cry tears of release, of freedom from pain
Weep for joys forgotten, for chances long past.
Cleanse the aches from your body, your soul
Live through your fears
To see a fresh scrubbed tomorrow.
Weep and be comforted as others weep with you.
Weep for inaction, lack of understanding, lack of love.
Weep because what we had was good.
It had its quiet pleasures
But that is gone...
Life became hollow, boring and dull.
That is why we weep.

Through the Century

PARENTS CONCERN

Where are you going?
And where have you been?
What time are you leaving?
What time do you get in?
Will you go by this way?
Can you bring me that?
What kind of clothes do you need?
Will you rent a flat?
These questions and more
Show a parent's concern.
They know we all have
So much more to learn.

Red Rock Canyon

MARRIAGES

You love me, you hate me,
You really don't care.
Who ever said marriages were wash and wear.
This one is full of wrinkles
Its had the odd tear
It's been mended and mended
But it's not beyond repair.
It's a natural fabric
Comfortable but not easy care.
You need to fuss a bit, fume a bit
Adjust, alter and change.
You're not the person I married.
Wow, did you change!
I'm not sure I like it—
But it's really not bad
On one side, I hate it
On the other, I'm glad.
Why do you bug me?
What's wrong with you?
Settle down—you're a clown
No, I'm really not fair
But life's never boring
With two of us there.
Why do you need me?
Why do I need you?
Do we really help
One another?
I get in such a stew!

10:30 pm

YOU CAN

You can, you can,
You really can!
Do it yourself
Believe and plan.
Don't be afraid,
Don't hesitate
Get out,
Get on with life
Before it's too late.
You know what you want
You can see it so plain.
If you just dream
It will all be in vain.
Picture it in detail
See the satisfaction and the joy.
Don't miss the challenge
Life's not a toy.
Create, create, communicate.
Mix and mingle
Go explore
Ideas come often on life's busy shore.
Keep yourself flexible
Bend and twist
Things are humorous
When seen like this.
From this angle
From that angle
From up and from down.
Flex, curl,
Give it a whirl
You can, you can, you really CAN!

Blackbird

THE RUBBLE

Climbing over the rubble of my life
Feeling the jagged rocks tear at me.
Some rocks worn smooth with time
Present themselves as wise choices
For rebuilding, recycling this life
Starting anew.
What changes will be made?
Not my friends—
They really know me—but, is that true?
I'm a strange combination
At times, too open—
At times, so well camouflaged
That even those I love haven't a clue.
Where does the agony come from?
The tears, the joy?
The struggle, the re-ordering?
Will the final product stand the test of time?
God, why am I so hard on me?
When will I ever learn—to just be?
I'm alone, so the tears can just roll down my face
Those few that I could share this with
I don't want to burden.
Some of the twisted girders will have to be replaced
But there's a window that survived!
The stained glass in it I always did prize.

Now I can see what's salvageable
And what's not.
I'd better redesign on a more suitable plot.
I need something that is open, that's warm, that's free.
I need space for some clutter,
Some books, the odd tree.
And room for someone who may come, go, or stay.
There may be some times I still need to get far, far away.
There needs to be a place to study,
To think, to work, to play—
A little color,
Some memories to brighten a dull day.
It's strange the things that I cling to
What I discard, what I keep.

On the Move

THE ETERNAL PLAN

Do you remember me after Marcie died?
Where did I ever get this foolish pride?
My grief was so private,
I just couldn't share it.
It was a strange thing to feel I had the responsibility
to help others to bear it.
I used to cry when I was alone.
When no one else was even at home.
Maybe that was my way to atone
But I never really felt guilty—just so alone.
I loved her a lot.
What searching you go through
Trying to decide what you should feel
What is for now, what for later—
What is really real
How dare one question the Eternal Plan
Or judge the value of a short life span.
Some of us live like there's no tomorrow
No future joy, no future sorrow.
Who's to say what is best
Or who passes or fails the final test?

Sassy Sunflowers

LET GO

Let go! Relax! Enjoy!
Today has possibilities
A passing smile or wave
A phone call from a friend
A letter bringing news of someone at earth's end.
Today brings its new challenges
Other avenues to explore
It brings a time for accomplishment
A time for pleasures shared.
It may bring sorrows But we will handle those
Let go—be free of the future and especially free of the past.
Don't let old memories haunt you
Free yourself at last.
They are over and done with.
Let go—tomorrow will take care of itself
The past and future need put on a shelf.
Feel the cold, the warmth, the joy—
Each minute is like a new toy
Let go! Relax! Enjoy!

Winter Birches

TENSIONS

I am tired of this tension,
This lack of understanding
And the tightness—
The resistance that drives it home.
I am weary of trying to think, to sort, to plan—
And yet, I feel I must.
It is my own whims I distrust.
I want to be me—to be free.
What will happen?
Wait and see.
Like others, I really don't understand me.

Madrone

STOPPED

There is a numbness to my life, A frozen, timeless journey—
Going nowhere, doing nothing—stopped.
There is a great hollow ache
Echoing and re-echoing throughout the caverns of my being.
There is an emptiness, a hollowness, a numbness in my heart.
No feeling, no joy—only vast inner space—
An unfathomable, endless inner ocean
With tides of longing and despair.
I had a husband but no love
I had a child but it left home
I had reasons for life but they are gone.

Sea Pearls

WHY?

In some of my worst nightmares
I am alone, caught in a trap
I could have avoided if I hadn't been frozen,
unable to communicate, unable to move
To make decisions and to follow them through.
In some of my best dreams
I am busy, with friends, solving problems, facing challenges—
Exploring new areas, helping and understanding the world.

BUBBLE WRAP

How much more of my life can I avoid,
Encase in plastic, put on a shelf and store forever—
To be opened when I least expect it by some uninvited guest.

Arbutus Ridge

THE REBEL

She must not resist life.
That would be totally wrong.
Resisting made life difficult.
There was only one thing to do
And that was to let go.
All her life she had resisted.
Resisting the trap of a strangling love
Resisting the tight narrow life styles
Forced on one by society and friends
Even the weather she resisted—
Its cold, chill fingers in the winter
And its searing, shriveling summer heat.
She did not accept life as it came.
She resisted giving in to its great pleasures
Almost as much as she resisted its pain.
She fought organization, exercise and direction.
Her whole life seemed dedicated to a resistance of the
standard, the usual, the norm. She was a rebel.
This tight resistance had to go, go.
Could she never relax, unwind, accept?
Could she never?

Angles

KEEP TRYING

I've tried
And I've succeeded
And I can't be all that wrong
Have faith, have courage
Friendly support can make you strong.
Some doubt you, some are jealous
Some really can't quite figure out you.
A little vision, A strong commitment
Occasional success can make you shout.
A crazy idea, A simple sharing,
A lot grows out of simply caring. Reach out, Lend a hand—
Your idea may improve this community, this land.

Lush

FIREFLIES

Fireflies skimming over the lawn
Do they really flit from dusk to dawn?
Fireflies are very much like a smile
They light up their surroundings for a short while.
Truly, they are much more beautiful than bees
Fireflies bring joy to one's heart
From the world of nature of which we are a part.
Fireflies send signals about in the dark,
Here and there all over the park.
Sheets of lightning brighten the sky
Hurry fireflies, Hurry by.

Presence

COURAGE

Courage when your back is to the wall
Courage when you think you're going to fall
Courage when you have to fight the fire
Courage when there's others to inspire
Courage when the way is all uphill
Courage when the enemy is there still
Courage when you feel the intense pain
Courage so you can go on again, again.
Courage that's what life is all about
Courage you can hear the others shout—
COURAGE

Where Dreams Begin

AT OUR CABANA

Between the old Japanese woman
And the young Mexican girl
Developed a friendship
As lustrous as a pearl.
They didn't know each other's language
But their souls cried out with joy.
The depth of their caring
The depth of their love
Provided a shower of blessings
That fell from above.

Coquitlam River

Life is full of wonder
The sun, the cold, the birds, the bees,
A child fascinated by a bug in the weeds.

Remember you have a lot to give
Things unique, all your own.
Your warmth, Your kindness,
Your love.

BOOK 2

HOROSCOPIC CONFUSION

According to the Chinese horoscope
I'm a rabbit.
Born the end of January 1940,
1939 was the Rabbit's Year.
The Lunar New Year
Began February 8th that Year.
The Year of the Dragon
Not just any Dragon
But the Metal Dragon.
That sounds formidable!
In Japan they no longer
Use the lunar calendar,
So, I am a Dragon.
A friend of mine
Had my Horoscope,
Done in Taiwan.
They believe I am a Dragon
My Husband thinks,
Maybe hopes I'm a Rabbit.
After all, he is a Wood Dog.
Loyal but able to chase,
Even catch Earth Rabbits.
As for me
I am confused.

Some days I want to be a Dragon-
Powerful, influencing, dramatic,
Other times, I want to nurture
    people,
Others, along a cooperative path,
To hop from painting beauty,
To pushing change through
    protest,
To steadily move forward----still
    confused!
Who, what am I?

"Dark Waters"

ALONG THE GOLDSTREAM

In late Spring or late Fall
We often stop by on route to Saltspring-
To visit people, the folks who have forged
An enduring bond with us.
Goldstream is tucked between two hillsides.
It rambles along over stones between logs,
Mossy logs dappled by sunlight
That filters through the foliage,
The angle depending on the time of day.
My camera can hardly wait to get there,-
To record the amazing, stunningly beautiful scenes.
The call of nature to share the peace---
The glory of creation- the endless variety
Of soul searching, life supporting---joy,
We belong.

"GoldStream"

YOUNG WOMEN

Special young women
From all over the world
Searching for the way
Not any way
But the best way
To develop economic potential-
To use money, resources and people well.
To establish human rights
To assert them, maintain them,
And find peace.
Peace which is more---
More than an absence of conflict.
Peace which is developed
Through equality, self-development and love.

"Butterfly Maiden", SOLD

PERSEVERANCE

Yes, many times—many, many times—
We question our luck, our possibilities, our strength,
To carry on, to have the resolve, the endurance,
And then it comes creeping back,
Helping us fight the good fight-
Get to the finish line-To look back.
With pride or joy
Or just plain thankfulness.

"Towards the Tantalus Two"

ON THE MOVE

On the move
All of them
Following the leader
Over the endless hills
Crossing the cold streams
To the areas
Of barren tundra
That provide sustenance-
Hard earned-
Bits of lichen
Tufts of evergreens
Food to strengthen them:
To continue life's journey,
In the endless loop of Creation.

"On the Move". SOLD

SPRING

First mini daffodils
Then tiny irises bloom-
Soon stunning pink Rhodos
Attract the passersby.
Then the mauve azaleas
Followed by the reds-
Has us anticipating,
Lacy, blue hydrangea heads.
The dogwoods are over,
Japanese cherries, too---
The verbena's creamy clusters
Now fresh against the green,-
The wigelia's pink arched branches
Poke out in between.
Yes, the COVID's kept us housebound,
But the gardens still call---
We plant the seeds,
Pull out the weeds---
And are gateful most of all.

"Blossoms"

SOLITUDE

I don't like to be alone
Bad things had happened,
When there is no one to help me.
So, I always needed company-
Even if I just needed time to think,
To plan, to adjust.
When my first marriage
Was on the rocks,
I went to Japan where I
Only knew one person---
And her English was as bad,
As my Japanese. But, I wasn't alone…..
Motoko was the kindest, most loving person,
I've ever met.
From her I learned acceptance,
Caring and pure unselfish love.
It was amazing.
She knew my needs….
She saw my flaws….
And she kept me from all harm.
Her love was enough to teach me,
How to live, how to cope=
How to survive, to be strong---
To eat well, to exercise---
And to look after our world---
As she did mine

"Lynn Valley Memory"

NORTH LIGHT

What is the attraction---
The soft glimmer
Outlining the hills,
The hummocks
With wind swept
Struggling trees
That survive,
In this rocky
Almost barren landscape.
There is always something,
That draws us here---
No matter the season
Lights can be the reason

"North Light"

SPRING

Frost gone,
Dew on the lawn
Robins seeking
Snowdrops peeping-

Birds chirping
Breezes sigh.
Wisps off cotton
Passing by

Pollen floats
On the wind
Sneezes coming
From within

Dandelions
In the lawn
Weeds to pull,
From dawn to dark.

Weather changing everyday-
Will the warm spell really stay?

Pea shoots up,
Radishes, too.
That kale sure
Looks a little blue

Bulbs awaken,
From their sleep
Tulips radiant
Colours so deep.

Daffodils. And Hyacinths
Burst from the ground,
Scilla and Grape
Hyacinths
Along paths abound.

"Near Cache Creek"

AS A TEACHER

As a teacher you touch many lives. If you are lucky
Your paths will cross again, when time has passed.
You meet them serving In White Spot-
Another waiting for help
In emergency with her son
Some may always stay in contact-
By mail, by email or by stopping by.
How exciting it was in 2018,
After attending a funeral
For the mother of two students
From my class of '59-60-
To get together for dinner
With those students later.
But also, to get the email out of the blue
Did you teach in Bear Creek?
A Grade 1-8 one room school--- In a logging camp.
Our times there didn't overlap.
Mine from 1959 to 1963, -theirs from 1965 to 1972,
Then ten days later, another email---
Dear Miss Harper, from a student in Grade Four---
I look at this as a small miracle.
Yes, I changed my name when I married George.
But I threw the whole thing out-
In 1989-changing first, middle and last.
How did they find me?

"Bridal Veil Falls"

TEACHING

Back to teaching but times have changed.
My classes were all E.S.L.
At first. they came from Hong Kong.
Any English they knew had a British accent.
They were polite- shocked when,
I picked out the rare swear word.
They cooperated--- discovering early on
My boundaries, my limits.
Then the Taiwanese came-still respectful.
Then I moved to New Westminster's
Justice program—new needs, new expectations-
And please check your e-mail-- DAILY!
It took me a year or two,
To become comfortable—
To accept this new convenience.
At the same time
We did a lot of negotiation—
Studying-people skills, consensus building
And more.

"Roses on the wall"

LANGUAGES

The phone rang.
They said it was for me—
It couldn't be, Could it?
My Spanish was in its infancy.
But—yes, the call was for me.
Whoever it was spoke clearly—
My only confusion was,
With the time of the bus.
Was it doce -or douze?
I couldn't be sure what I had heard.
Should I meet the bus at two or at twelve?
That was long ago---it turned out fine.
With foreign languages
One needs to listen carefully—
Ma? A horse, a mother or what in Chinese.
I remember a recent faux-pas
When I said Motoko was my Onni-sama---My devil
Not my Onne-sama my big sister—
Fortunately, she understood.
All her friends laughed with us.

"Continental Colour"

LOST

Lost on the path of life-
Unable to decide-what to value,
What to share, who to trust
Who really cares.
What makes a difference-
What doesn't matter.
Somethings are so tempting,
Others too simple, too plain-
To be treasured
But possibly- the best value-
Even something we need.
Don't lose your sense of humor,
Don't lose your fascination with learning-
With caring and gentleness.
The path will become obvious soon.

"Lonesome Lake"

INTOLERANCE

Stomp out intolerance.
But, do it softly, gently-
So they become more open,
More accepting, more understanding.
Broaden the parameters,
Of their perception.
Help them to see-
There is no need for fear.
Everyone has something,
To give, to share.
Some of the weirdest people
Suddenly shine lights on baffling challenges-
An insight that leaves others
In awe.
Where this kind of revelation
Comes from---
Is part of life's mystique.
Where would our world be without them?

"Soda Pop Falls"

SEEKING PRIVACY

Some place to confront ones' self-
With no interference—from anyone—
Not my friends, not my relations
Just a place to peer inside me.
To decide what I could do—
What I should do—for me.
To be meaningful, satisfactory-
Wanting to be useful, helpful—
To be empowering
For others
Yet—
To be comfortable, knowing—
Somehow understanding
My needs—
Possibly to share—
To be content with my lot—
At this point in time.

"Madeira Morning"

BURNS BOG

Slush, gush, mush—the forest grows lush.
Brown, brackish river through a cranberry bog,
Mist creeping, sun peeping, through the coming fog.

Brambles, bracken, bushes and bog-
Cedar shake blocks, pole or log-
Waterfall tumbling, slow moving stream-
Dragonflies, waterbugs, part of a dream
Bullrushes, cattails—misty March morning
Tree frogs, lily pads, minnows and more.
Stellar Jays darting, bald eagles soaring-
Otters playing,--salmon maybe praying.

"Burns Bog"

MY MONSTERS

My children were my 'monsters',
My nephews they were 'things'.
What a lot of wonderful memories
These terms bring.
Thing three and thing four
Usually met me at the door.
They'd laugh and hoot—
Introducing me as a 'thing' to boot.
And when I queried Nancy
Asked if she'd ever been a brat—
She said she'd always been a monster,
And she'd prefer to leave it at that.

"The Campsite"

SISTERS

I have many sisters,
In all walks of life.
Some have had an easy life-
Others faced nothing but strife.
Some have an inner glow,
And you welcome these with ease-
Others are jealous or suspicious-
These you rarely please.

"Atlin Autumn"

LIFE

Seeing the joy in all creation
Seeing the challenges facing the nation—
Seeing the hardships-
The weary, the worn, the beaten
Seeing life taking its toll.
Seeing success, friendship and love-
Love for all creation-
The strong, the weak, the shy, the bold.
Accepting life and carrying on,
Trying to teach people to be positive, strong.
Celebrating accomplishments-.
Enjoying life.
We have to work to end the strife.
And make the time to celebrate life.

"Fantasy Forest"

MUSIC

Listen to the music, not the words-
Especially if the words are foreign-
Or totally indistinct.
The music or tone
Will lead you to understanding.
So I was advised before
I went to my first operatic performance.
Yes, the music by itself,
Can lift you up or wear you down-
Interpreting the suggested story
Will keep your imagination,
Running full speed or—
At least at the pace of the music,
Whether it is a solo or a whole gamelan orchestra—
Excellent advice for anyone especially crossing cultures.
Just ENJOY!

"Crescendo"

RESPECT

Who should we respect?
Anyone who earns our respect?
Including all races, all colours, all creeds-
But what about the ones who disappoint you?
Do you continue to respect them?
Can you really love them,
If you don't respect them?
Yes, you can tolerate them-
Give them a second or third chance-
But if disappointment,
Follows disappointment-
Eventually you will find reasons,
To distance yourself from them-
To keep other company
Company that keeps their word
That indicate your voice,
Has been heard-
That your needs will be met,
That they will not forget.

"Edge of the Woods"

LISTENING

Listening
Consciously-to the rhythmic pace
The inflection, the tone
Unable to discern,
The precise meaning
But—listening as one does
To a symphony for the first time
Trying to catch the emotions,
To discern the purpose
The reason behind the language,
The speech
Listening as one does to the rain.
The steady flow
The stormy punctuation
The messages received,
Some comforting
Others carry warnings,
Wordlessly alerting us
To the state of our surroundings
Be aware— NOW!

"Asian Gold"

ICE STORM

Have you ever been in an ice storm?
It happens when the temperature variation,
Changes the cold rain,
Freezing it to coat everything it contacts.
It becomes a crystal clear decoration,
Imagine tree branches,
Even the smallest ones coated with ice.
Prisms of light dancing everywhere
Diamond topped tiaras on small branches,
Looking out from within the wonderland
Is too beautiful for words.
Better not venture outside,
Everywhere is a skating rink
Especially the highway.
Stay home.
As the weather changes the weight of the ice
Will break the branches, crack tree trunks,
Some flexible saplings will stay bent
For the rest of their lives.
Ice storms can be awesome,
Picturesque, powerful and fearsome.

"Ice Storm"

THE STAG

It is funny how the past,
Creeps back into our worlds.
Heading out after school
To chop down a tree
To fill the wood box,
I stopped half-way,
Aware of the stag
In the neighboring meadow—
Tall, regal—
Perusing its surroundings,
It made a lasting impression-
Revised by Sir Walter Scott's
The Stag at Eve
And again, one night at the singles dance-
Noticing Bill's perusal of the dance floor-
There he was again---
The Stag at Eve.

"Sidehill Show"

THE CRITIC

As children our parents are our main critics.
Their way of coaching us, disciplining us
May set our ability to accept criticism throughout our lives.
Criticism balanced with encouragement or positivity,
Will help us develop our strengths.
Our next critics could be our neighbours or close relatives.
Then come our teachers.
The influence these people
Have on our lives is immense.
It may be a casual comment that sets us off on a new path-
Of exploration of exciting possibilities—
Of a chance to create, to achieve status,
To become the best person possible.
Being a critic is having power.
Power to encourage excellence—
To avoid disappointment—
To see the struggles and possible outcomes—
To focus on what can be.

"Retired"

REFLECTIONS

Where was the power?
Was it with the Maya,
Who created the pyramid and left?
Or the climate change,
That forced their relocation?
Relocation that let the jungle reclaim the area—
Creeping over the pyramids
Clothing them in greens of every shade.
The jungle of Tikal took over—
Mayan pyramids, Aztec ones, too.
It wasn't selective.
We wandered-climbed some pyramid—
Until we were above the treetops.
Watching the spider monkeys—
Swing from tree to tree—
Were we powerful?
Were we free?

"Reflections"

CHAINS

Chains of life, chains of love-
Chains for safety, chains for torture-
Chains for a short time, chains for eternity,
Chains of memories, chains from above-
Chain of connections, Chain of command—
Chains around your wrist
Chained hand to hand-
Chained to your work,
Chained to your land.
It all comes back to the chain of command.
Chained to the future, chained to the past-
Live in the present—chain free at last.

"Fulford Harbour"

SEEDS

Seeds are set out in the Spring,
Not knowing what the weather may bring.
Like ideas, small suggestions
That may encounter rock like obstacles,
Due to poor presentation skills
Or lack of tact.
If the ideas are timely
They may become catch phrases,
For improving life, society.
If the reception is positive, sunny-
With a little humour, even funny—
They may grow rapidly,
But without the right conditions
They may be a flash in the pan.
If many love the idea
It can grow like the well-nourished seed,
And change society at an amazing speed.
Small ideas can change the world-
Simple things—like the song of a bird.

"Farm Fields"

BELIEFS

Whatever you believe, will empower your journey.
If you belong to a gang that believes
Rich people do not deserve to be rich-
You won't feel bad about robbing them.
If you believe all people and animals should be cared for,
You will try to keep them healthy and happy.
If you believe that nature—all plants, all animals-
Every species has rights-
You will try to make their world better.
If you believe your life counts-
You can make a difference.
If you believe you have no value
You will suffer and suffer.
Empowering youth to walk on
A path of caring and strength
Is a job for all of us.
Everyone has something to give—
And everyone needs to belong.

"By the Steam"

NEAR AND FAR

I moved—
Away from my parents, my family, my friends.
Starting over at seventeen in a new city,
A new neighborhood, a new school, a new job.
Moving three maybe four times that year—
Then to UBC—a new family, a new system, new friends.
Followed by a job teaching—18 miles from Harrison-
By air or water—REMOTE.
A new start,--
About twenty families, sixteen to nineteen students.
I was the teacher, the principal, and janitor.
In a one room, Grade 1 to 8 school.
I was on my own—no one to guide me.
I had so much to learn-
At nineteen.

"Arctic Summer"

TO BE OR NOT TO BE

To reach out-
To get along
To find solutions-
It won't take long
To respect all;
To include all,
To tell our stories,
To share our lives-
To work together
Like in a hive.
To influence others,
To share our expertise,
To be fearlessly authentic,
To be principled, even daring
Remember to listen, to thrive.
To understand how best to be alive-
To help conquer the world's ills—
To leave a legacy and empower—
Still complicated, beautiful humans.

"Mirage"

DECISIONS

Most of us make many serious decisions in our lifetimes,
We may stew over them; postpone them or have no time for either of these.
Accidents happen, serious illnesses may arrive—time may be limited to now.
If you must, you must and you live with your decision.
Sometimes, you share the load.
Trying to help my child, a teenager, for her future,
I sent her to the doctor on her own—The doctor, a young lady at the beginning of her practice-
Marcia, who I had instructed to get an appointment with an eye doctor,
Had done that but she was frustrated by the doctor.
She said, "I'll never see that doctor again."
She had been told "many teenagers have headaches." Nothing more.
Next, we went to the eye doctor at 11am.
We were sent to the neurologist at 1pm.
We had the appointments for an angiogram and CT scan the next day.
She was hospitalized after she was told she had a brain tumor.
She saw the neurosurgeon. They talked.
She agreed to the operation.
I asked God to do what was best for her—to keep her alive if that was best-
But to let her go if she would be in constant pain,
and we would suffer watching her suffer.
She lived through the surgery but only overnight.
She left us but we believe she is our guardian angel.
One who takes good care of us.

"Sunset Sentinals"

THE BURDEN

Shouldering the burden of being
Being able to help others,
Having trod similar steps,
Provides a way to guide others,
To help them survive the worst.
To find ways of acceptance
Of our differences
To accept foreign beliefs.
To patch flaws in understanding.
To bridge the abyss
From which they hope to climb,
But needing the tools, the techniques,
The awareness of the possible,
The route to community—
To belonging—
To being part of we/us.

"Salish Sea Sunset"

WIND, WATER, WEATHER, WHAT, WHY, WHERE

Any place else----just not HERE.
Our beautiful, peaceful forests
Burnt—gone.
Months after the fires
The atmospheric Rivers came.
Drenching the hillsides-
Tearing at the skeletons of trees
Until the weight moved them
Downhill with the downpour
Down, down, down.
Destroying the roads, the bridges,
Blocking transport of food, help, necessities—
Access to homes, to loved ones, to hope.
We have changed the earth
BUT not for the better—
Will we really survice?

"Mystic Mountains"

ITS ABOUT TIME

It's about time we change direction-
Start to value life on earth,
All life, no matter—
The colour, the race, the birth.
Be good to each other-
We have the same need-even though-
We don't come from the same seed.
If the earth is preserved—
All the air, all the oceans, all the lands
We should be a much happier band.
We should be cooperative.
With those in desperate need—
Especially the mothers
With many mouths to feed.
At times like these-
where there is too much stress-
Helping out,---sharing a friendly shout-
Will go a long way to banish the pain.
To help them smile.
When staying in, out of the rain.

"Winter Wonderland"

THE FLICKER

We came home from shopping,
Parked the car—
Noticed the young flicker.
It sat, not moving—
Like a perfect statue
Not a feather out of place.
We were struck by the awesome presence,
Of the motionless bird.
Eventually, Bill decided,
To open his car door.
Startled the bird took flight
--not high—just away.
The flash of underwing orange
Carrying us away, too.
Awed by the beauty,
The perfect markings,
The regal presence visiting us-
For that unforgettable moment of time.

"The Visitor"

MORNING LIGHT

Mid-morning crossing the deck.
I am drawn in by the sun,
Announcing its presence
By gilding the tops of the clouds
That ran across the sky layer on layer.
Pushing the high rises on the far shore
to reveal their imperial presence-
Before dumping the leftover gift
Now silver
Onto the river below
The silver contrasting with the dark greens
Of the evergreens on the northern shore.
I ran for my camera,
Hoping the light would stay-
Long enough for me to catch it, keep it,
Treasure its celebration-
Of life.

"On the Quay"

FEATHERED FRIENDS

The blue jays have gone.
This year they moved half a block south.
Perhaps they now live
In the big cedar tree on Ladner Street.
Perhaps they feel safer there-
Hidden from those pesky crows.
Perhaps we just don't know.
No birds live in our apple tree now.
Bill had it pruned back severely-
So, we content ourselves,
With the chatter of finches
In the hedgerow near our bedroom window.
It seems every Spring a couple
Build a home in the hedge.
Then for several weeks
Every morning the male sits in the lilac
And flies up bumping the window,
With its chest. Bumping again and again.
He demands our attention. We cannot ignore him.
Several weeks later he stops. He is a strange performer.
WHY?

"Salt Spring Sidehill"

- BEFORE

Before he was a grandfather
> He was retired, no longer a log trader.

Before he met Roxsane
> He played slow pitch with a much younger crowd.

Before he quit playing golf
> He walked with ease, hiked the forests.

Before he took a Mediterranean Cruise
He travelled Ireland by bus and drove us around the indigenous
> SouthWest.

Before he settled in with Roxsane
> He played bridge with the ladies.

Before he left Al Anon
> He learned a broader acceptance and understanding.

Before his children married
He hoped for grandchildren and became an adopted Grandfather,
Before his grandchildren arrived
> Walking became a challenge, playing hide and seek was difficult.
Life is not Fair.

"Salmon Stream"

DAWNING

Crammed with activities,
Overflowing exertion
Getting the vegetables
Gleaned from the garden yesterday.
Scrubbing, peeling, chopping,
Making the broth.
Soup would come later-
After the emails were read
After the cheque details were found
After the poster was printed
After the writing class—
Soup for supper or lunch?
What kind? Lentil? Bean?
Or turkey based—
Soup—one of the strengths
Of a waste not, want not life.

"Helen's Hideaway"

A TRUE FRIEND

If you are a true friend
A true friend of mine
You'll explain Your different thoughts,
And I'll explain mine
Together we'll make progress,
In peace and harmony
And good things will follow,
For all to see.
We both want the best of worlds,
We want our group to prosper—
Steadiness and honesty
Are the best I've got to offer.
The process must be open,
Nothing should be hidden.

"Northern Lights"

QUIETLY GRATEFUL

For the love notes
Left beside my bed in the early morning,
While I sleep, continue to sleep.
Awaken to find the note-
The crossword on the table-
Hot water and lemon,
Slightly cooled.
I am spoiled and I know it.
The cheery Good Morning
From Nancy
The always available
Cup of hot water-
The precious time
Just to talk-With Pat,
Or maybe to walk. The many gifts of time
      Of conversation
      Of companionship
      Of two-way support and caring
A huge network of friends, extended family
Always expanding
Always a treasure
With insights into the modern world from the very young.

"Statice"

LOVE

Did you ever try to put love in a freezer?
To keep it, ignore it
Till you want to unstore it?
Did you put it in there-
Out of the way, out of your hair-
Till you decide it is time to share.
NOT FAIR!
Did you try to take a little leftover love
To warm it up
To heat it gently
To honestly strive to keep it alive—
To want it to grow-
Because you need love so-
Did you ever try to put love in a cup
To sip it slowly so it can warm you up-
So that famous elixir
Is what you have to fix'er
What have you done with my love?

"Cathy's Garden"

AUTUMN

Every autumn we travel in search of colour,
We chase Jack Frost's magic=
In the colour of the trees.
Thus our annual pilgrimages
To the Yukon, to Algonquin park, to Whistler-
Anywhere the scenery bids us go.
Like gypsies we follow
the burble of small streams
The echo of canyons
The contrasts that say we belong
Watching the swaying dance
Of the leaves before they depart.
Celebrating another year
Before being trapped by the cold.

"Lost Lagoon"

BARRIERS

Barriers made by others,
Barriers to the truth
To a fulfilling life.
Being too young, to naïve
To know where or how
To get help, support-
For a way to stay healthy, alive.
Dishonesty all around
Fear of saying anything, anything
For fear of cutting all ties-
Of everyone thinking
Your version was lies-
Attention getting lies,
So you swallow hard
Bite your tongue,
Pour your frustration,
Into pure physical labour
While your shell thickens
While you focus on one goal—
Survival -maybe even freedom.

"Deek's Creek"

WORDS

Sometimes there are no words—
None to describe the depth of the cold.
The lack of reasonable warmth,
The feelings of being outside-
Of being ostracized-
Indefensible.
Uncooperative,
Unneeded.
And more.
You need words to educate,
To share, to create hope,
Ambition and love of life
You need words to show you care,
To empower, to accept, to befriend.
Learning words, expressions
There may be misunderstandings,
Cross cultural confusions and all.
But the attempts
Lead to mutual efforts—
To paths, bridges and caring-
Caring for all.

"Coastal Colour"

RIVER

River dance, river prance
Take me down to the sea.
River run, river fun,
Where will the best spot be?

River of dreams,
River of thought
River of motion
River of nought.

River flow,
River go—
To the sea of tranquility.
River cry-
River fly
Through canyon walls so high.

River of dreams-
Not what it seems-
River of life-
Some peace, some strife.
River of love,
Sent from above.

"Red Rock Rapids"

OUR NEEDS

I belong in the moss laden forests of British Columbia
Near a small stream, a place where the wild things live.
A place to observe, to listen, to dream of peace,
Of a welcoming world unsullied by man.
In his greed, his need for possessions.
His limited vision—
His search for one kind of wealth at the cost of another
Forgetting the animals, their space, their needs—
My needs, our needs----still.

"Heron Deer Lake"

BUTTERFLIES

Tens, hundreds, thousands, millions--
in the air,
On the flowers, on the path, on the trees.
There were everywhere-the Monarchs
In their glorious colours
In their gentle softness
Their very fragility.
The awe,
The sense of wonder,
the heavenly peace.
A once in a lifetime experience.
The voices hushed or silent
the vanishing of self
The all-encompassing sense
of balance, of communication.
of shared energies, shared breaths,
Shared oneness.
Enough for all.
At Rosario, the UN sponsored site
high in the pine and spruce forests of Mexico.

"Perennial Preview"

FOCUS

It is a beautiful, sunny day.
The crocuses and daffodils
Are poking through-
Showing the world
They are survivors.
They greet us,
To show us the way
To warm people's hearts-
To create unusual art-
To give us much needed
Hope—inspiring visions
Of a better world-
A place of justice,
Of calm, of equality
And appreciation
For all efforts to
See the big picture.
To help wherever possible,
To encourage, to support,
To understand.
Not to punish, not to destroy,
Whether boys or girls,
Women or men-
Focus on the positive,
Again, and again.

"Autumn Acres"

STANDING IN THE FOREST

Soaking up the beauty, the silence
Escaping the cacophony of traffic-
The chatter of the playground-
The words flung in anger,
That drove you to the solace,
The comfort of the trees.
How fortunate to be able,
To get here so quickly
To view the stillness of the lake,
The fallen logs, the water lilies-
After some minutes passed
To be finally interrupted
By the call of the Jay—
Carried by the breeze,
That ripples the water.

"Forest Retreat"

WHAT?

What did you notice?
The blue jays in the apple tree-
The white moths on the broccoli
The prolific blackberries-
Sending out shoots-
Five feet long!
The gogi berries parading
Along the stalks
How important it is
To get out and WALK.
What did you hear?
The cacophony of the pile driver,
The constant hum of the street cleaner,
The rare sirens heading to the hospital;
And the quiet before the STORM.
What did you admire?
The people who thought to call the elderly once a week.
Having tea on the deck with social distancing and respect.
Consideration for others -and generosity of SPIRIT.
What astonished you?
The smoke from California-
The visiting birds eating seeds from the verbena TREE.
What would you like to see again?
The young flicker on the fence post by the lane-
The comical rare spotted squirrel in his Sunday best.
And the didactic crows protecting their NEST.
What was the most wonderful?
The gentle breeze
Just enough to refresh us in the heat.
The fellows working hard,
To make the neighbour's yard neat.
And of course, the fresh blackberry ice cream TREAT.

"Gold Stream Morn"

TRACING LOSS

There was no preparation,
      For the loss-
No time to learn acceptance-
To develop thoughts—
To live with the absence
Of laughter, of need-,
The departure was swift,
The space evacuated-
Missing key components-
Gone.
The second time
      Wasn't easier.
It was sudden!
Shocking
Almost unbelievable.
Even though—
It had to be true.
Their spirits joined together,
Seven years later.
At times we feel flickers
Of remembrance—
Of support, of caring--,
Ethereal...........-

"The Hobbit Tree"

LUCIE

We did not have to ask for Lucie's friendship, her caring
Her ability to make her students blossom.
Feeling her belief in them,
Her over-powering confidence
That their lives had meaning.
That she reached out
With hope and later with joy
Seeing the results of her efforts.
Lucie's presence warmed all her world.
She had patience learned through a war-torn childhood
In the Netherlands.
She had courage earned through the large and small trials of life.
That she overcame
Bouncing back with a smile,
gentle laughter
And a wise sense of humour.
She had many special abilities
She spoke Dutch, --of course
And French and English all well.
She was also a painter, an artist, an observer of life.
That she sprinkled with her music
Getting us together to sing after school
Accompanying us on her guitar.
We got together often
After all she was the magnet
Drawing us in—inspiring us
Encouraging our efforts to make our world better
Step by step.
Lucie is IN THE SKY WITH DIAMONDS.
She will outshine them all. Thank you for sharing her.

"Winter Wonderland"

MARIE ROSE

The strength of character
The open acceptance of others—
Their twists and turns.
Her very positive, gentle, steady way
Of dealing with life's challenges-
She learned to bring out the best in people.
To live with the technical advances as they came-
To offer help whenever she could.
As a farmer's wife
She prepared food for harvesters-
Woke up early in calving time.
She never turned a guest away.
She gardened, canned, or pickled—
Food was never a problem.
Marie Rose was a beautiful person.
Inside and out. We all enjoyed her company.
Now the angels will.

We will miss her.
We will miss her.

"Manitoba Thaw"

ABOUT THE AUTHOR

Roxsane was born and raised in the Greater Vancouver area.

She became an international educator, teaching high school and marketing for the district in Korea, Taiwan, Hong Kong, Japan and Mexico. Wherever she travels she soaks up local colour, customs and cultural influences. The cross-cultural experiences blend with her lively imagination, her creativity and her love of the outdoors provide an endless variety of subjects for her art work. Now, she lives in Burnaby.

One afternoon in Japan, in 1984, she took a class in Chigiri-e a Japanese torn paper collage technique. This opened her creative channels. Now, she enjoys the variety of paper—the feel of it. It can be sturdy or fragile, bright or hazy, fibrous or sheer-gauzy. She loves it all.

Recently, she is exploring the vibrant, audacious color of acrylics. Often she combines them with paper to create a mixed media piece. She has been a member of the Burnaby Artists Guild for over twenty yeas helping with the creation of mosaic murals for the Tommy Douglas Library and BC Children's Hospital.

Roxsane is an energetic 83 year old. She has caring, community-oriented siblings, two wonderful daughters, five grandchildren and a one year old great grandson. Her wide circle of friends is scattered all over the globe, and at home she has a wonderful man named Bill who makes her life complete.

Roxsane's early life was challenging but she completed he teacher's training at UBC, taught in a one room school on Harrison Lake and married George Dheilly. Together they raised three beautiful daughters. The youngest died of brain tumour in 1981. Their marriage fell apart in 1983-1984. Needing to find more meaning in her life, after the girls left home, she decided to go back to university to complete her Bachelor of Education and get back to the most meaningful career she could find---teaching at the High School Level. Since then she has worked in Mexico for the World Association of Girl Guides and Girl Scouts, traveled extensively and taught International Students and immigrants before retiring, becoming a capable author and artist.

In my travels and through life every time I enter a place of worship for the first time, I ask For understanding or wisdom. They are gifts we all need. The content of my poems reflect What I have learned—Roxsane Tiernan

www.ingramcontent.com/pod-product-compliance
Lightning Source LLC
Chambersburg PA
CBHW051143120626
46547CB00012B/926